THE
PRINCIPLES
OF
Prayer

THE PRINCIPLES OF PRAYER
2nd Edition

by Jacqueline Bell

© Copyright by Jacqueline Bell, 2023
All Rights Reserved

All Scripture quotations, unless otherwise stated, are from the King James Version of The Bible.

Cover Design: RAW Design Studios
designzbyraw.com
ryan@designzbyraw.com

Editor-in-Chief: Minister Patrick Henry, M.A., M.A., LPC

3P: PH Pentecostal Publishing, LLC
New Albany, OH
3ppublish.weebly.com

This text is available NOW on Amazon!

Dedication

I dedicate this book to the memory of my husband, Bishop D. Rayford Bell, Th.D., Ph.D.

Acknowledgments

I would like to thank my Lord and Savior, Jesus Christ, for the inspiration to write and complete this publication. Also, I would like to thank Bishop J.E. Moore, Ph.D., Ph.D., for his wisdom to help make a difficult task easier. Finally, I would like to thank my friend, Patrick, my daughter, Carmen, and my grand-daughter, Navee. I sincerely appreciate your help.

CONTENTS

Introduction
The Direct Access of Prayer: The Veil is TORN!

Mankind has not always had direct access to God. From the Fall of Adam in the Garden of Eden until Calvary, mankind had limited access to God. From Enoch, to Noah, Abraham and the rest of the patriarchs and prophets of the Old Testament, God selectively engaged in intimate fellowship almost exclusively with leaders.

Regarding the sacrificial system of the Old Testament, only the Jewish high priest had direct access to God through his service in the Temple. The high priest, as mandated by God Himself, could only enter the Holy of Holies (or Most Holy Place) once per year. The purpose was to offer sacrifices for the sins of the entire Jewish congregation, including himself. The only separation between the Holy of Holies and the inner court of the tabernacle was a tall, thick veil. If, on account of his own sins or some other error of the people, the high priest's offering was unacceptable to God two tragedies took place. First, the high priest would die instantly. Second, the congregation would be forced to wait an entire year before the next high priest had the opportunity to approach God once again on behalf of the people to make temporary atonement for Israel.

Other than the high priests, we have Biblical record that certain spiritual leaders also had direct access to God. God hand-selected men and a few women with whom to bond intimately. Men such as David, Samuel, Isaiah, Jeremiah etc. were able to enjoy the privilege of close contact with God. Everyone else, while they may talk to God privately, often had to rely upon the chosen high priest or these leaders (kings and prophets) to receive any communication from God.

However, when the fullness of time had come, here comes the Savior: Jesus Christ. He was born of a woman and yet eternal. He was born under the Mosaic Law, and yet He was the very fulfillment of the Law. At Calvary, Jesus became all sin in the sense that He bore mankind's sins in His flesh, although He never sinned. By bearing our sins and dying a real physical death, Jesus, in essence, destroyed our collective sins. His flesh became sin. Jesus' flesh can be likened unto the sin of mankind, which in turn, can be likened unto the veil that separated the inner court from the Most Holy Place (see Hebrews 10:20). Therefore, once Jesus' flesh was destroyed by death, so was the veil of sin separating mankind from God! My Lord...what a Savior!

Now we can access God directly. Thus, the Hebrew writer beseeches us to come boldly to the throne of grace. That boldness is not irreverence, but it merely underscores the clear spiritual reality that we can enjoy the privilege of direct access to Jesus - regardless of our spiritual standing, leadership status, race, class, finances, gender, etc. Hallelujah! Anyone can speak directly to God and He can and will speak directly back to us, because He promises to hear our prayers. There is no need to wait one year for the human high priest to commune with God on our behalf.

So, I implore everyone who reads this book. Pray to Jesus incessantly! Pray properly! Teach others to do likewise! Follow this and you (and those whom you impact) will prosper!

PS - This book is a manual. It is a guide for readers to use in order to teach themselves and/or others basic principles governing prayer. As such, this book allows room for teachers of prayer to utilize this text as a foundation for teaching prayer, at the individual, familial, and corporate levels. Each lesson begins with a 1-3 page summary which explains the gist of the lesson, followed by a brief outline which instructors can use to teach the principles of that lesson. Finally, there is a summary at the end of each lesson listing key points from that particular lesson.

Grace & Peace Unto You & Yours,

Minister Patrick Henry, M.A., M.A., LPC

Lesson 1: Examine Yourself
Introduction

The *"Prayer Evaluation"* questionnaire, has been placed at the beginning of this book because it is always in our best interest to know where we stand spiritually in our relationship with the Lord.

Examine yourselves, whether ye be in the faith; prove your own selves know ye not your own selves, how that Jesus Christ is in you...? **II Corinthians 13:5**

In this scripture, the Corinthians were questioning Paul's proof of Christ's speaking in him, however, it was by his ministry that they believed in the first place. Paul withstood their questioning, and asked them to "examine themselves," as to whether they were acting in the Christian Faith.

All professing Christians should *examine themselves*, regarding the reality of their present salvation.

For I say, through the grace given unto me, to every man that is among you, not to think of himself more highly than he ought to think; but to think soberly... **Romans 12:3**

One might believe that they are doing well in their spiritual walk, but upon closer examination, we might find the contrary. Many people think, for example, that they *already know how to pray*, and therefore they do not find it necessary to be taught how to pray.

Spiritual check-ups or examinations have rewarding benefits:

- Helps us to face the truth

- Allows us to recognize our strengths and weaknesses

- Reveals where organization and priorities are needed

- A reminder to stay focused

Maybe it's not a bad idea to have an annual or semi-annual check-up to prevent spiritual illnesses that will hinder our prayers. Let's be honest, and let's get started!

Examine Yourself
Evaluation

Below are 10 questions that will help you evaluate your Prayer Life. If you give sincere and honest answers, you will get an accurate picture of your true relationship with the Lord. Each "yes" answer is worth 10 points, and each "no" answer is worth 0 points. The total possible points are 100.

Ask yourself the following:

1. __Yes __No   Is praying a privilege to me and not an obligation?

2. __Yes __No   Is my mind (consciousness) focused on the Lord when I pray?

3. __Yes __No   Am I aware of the Holy Spirit's presence when I pray?

4. __Yes __No   Do I begin my prayer with thanksgiving and praise, to invite His presence?

5. __Yes __No   Do I **overcome** an improper attitude and laziness that attempt to hinder my prayers?

6. __Yes __No   Do I have a **set time** and **set place** to meet God **daily**?

7. __Yes __No   As a result of my prayer life, have I noticed changes in my life?

8. __Yes __No   Do I have set times for fasting and praying for spiritual purposes?

9. __Yes __No   Am I reading the Word of God **daily** to be sure I am praying according to the will of God?

10. __Yes __No   Do I give testimony to the glory of God for answering my prayer(s)?

Total Score: _____

Summary

- Check-ups help us to face the truth about our spirituality.

- Self-examination allows us to recognize our strengths and weaknesses.

- Self-examination reveals where distinct priorities and greater organization are needed.

- Check-ups remind us to stay focused on guarding our spiritual life.

Lesson 2: Why Pray?
Introduction

Why don't some people pray? Here are several reasons why some people don't pray:

- some don't know how to pray;

- some don't believe God will hear and answer their prayers;

- some don't believe He is able to answer their requests;

- some believe God seems too distant;

- some question the existence of God;

- some feel God doesn't really care enough to intervene on their behalf;

- some don't see the difference it makes;

- some think it's boring.

These reasons couldn't be further from the truth. Let me encourage you, nothing is too hard or too difficult for God (Genesis 18:14; Ephesians 3:20). God does care and desires to meet our every need (Philippians 4:19; I Peter 5:7). We must correct our thinking, and then we will be free to seek Him in prayer (Proverbs 23:7; Romans 12:2). God is waiting to hear from you (Jeremiah 33:3)! In this lesson, we hope to give you some serious reasons to pray that we hope will inspire and ignite a desire in you to spend more time in prayer.

First and foremost, prayer is a privilege! It is a privilege to go to God in prayer. The mere fact that a Holy, Omnipotent, and Eternal God is available, willing, and eager to fellowship and commune with us is an amazing privilege. Jesus' sacrificial death on the cross paid the price for us to be able to have access into His presence. Let us not waste this privilege!

There is an old familiar song written by Joseph Scriven in 1855, called "What a Friend We Have in Jesus!" The lyrics tell us why we should pray. As you read the words to this hymn, feel the profound willingness of the Father to hear our prayers, and the loving concern of the Father.

Song: "What a Friend We Have in Jesus"

What a Friend we have in Jesus, All our sins and griefs to bear!

What a privilege to carry, Everything to God in prayer!

O what peace we often forfeit, O what needless pain we bear,

All because we do not carry, Everything to God in prayer!

Have we trials and temptations? Is there trouble anywhere?

We should never be discouraged, Take it to the Lord in prayer.

Can we find a friend so faithful, Who will all our sorrows share?

Jesus knows our every weakness, Take it to the Lord in prayer.

Are we weak and heavy laden, Cumbered with a load of care?

Precious Savior, still our refuge, Take it to the Lord in prayer.

Do thy friends despise, forsake thee? Take it to the Lord in prayer,

In His arms He'll take and shield thee, thou wilt find a solace there.

Do you take everything to God in prayer? A great sin of God's people is living independently of their God! He delights in knowing our desires and needs, but God waits for us to ask Him so that He can act on our behalf. That's **why we pray**!

Why Pray?
Outline

I.   **Prayer is a *privilege.***

    a. Definition of *privilege:*   a special right or advantage; to grant someone special favor.

    b. As referenced in the Introduction of this book, the curtain or veil separating the Holy Place from the Most Holy Place barred the way into the presence of God. Yet, the tearing of the veil of the temple after the death of Christ signified that the way has now been opened into the presence of God.

    c. Jesus Christ died for this privilege. Through the death of Christ, the curtain was removed and the way into the most Holy Place (God's presence) was opened for all who believe in Christ (Matthew 27:51; Hebrews 10:19-22).

    d. Our access is gained through Christ and specifically through His shed blood on the cross (Ephesians. 2:13-14, 18).

    e. Christ is now our High Priest, opening a way to His personal presence whereby we can always seek the help we need (Hebrews. 4:14-16; Hebrews 6:20).

II.   **Prayer is a *commandment.***

    a. Definition of *commandment:* an order given by authority

    b. Believers are commanded to pray and not faint! We must acquire a serious life of prayer or we will become spiritually weak (Luke 18:1; Ephesians 6:18; Philippians. 4:6)!

c. God needs our prayers. God gave mankind the authority to determine what happens on earth (Genesis 1:26). God does nothing on earth without the cooperation of a person (II Chronicles 7:14; Ezekiel 22:30-31; Matthew 7:7-8; Matthew 16:19; Monroe, 2002).

d. How can we say we love God and not pray (John 14:15; John 15:10)?

III. **Prayer is a *spiritual relationship*.**

a. Definition of *relationship*: the state of being connected by blood or marriage

b. God desires our fellowship, and by prayer we maintain our relationship with Him. Prayer is the lifeline to our spiritual life.

c. God communicates with us through our spirit.

d. Supporting verses: Genesis 2:7; John. 3:3-8; John 4:23-24; Romans 8:26-27; I Corinthians 2:9-14

IV. **Prayer is a *foundation* of the Church.**

a. Definition of *foundation*: base of a building, that by which anything stands, or is supported

b. The four foundations of the Church are: doctrine, fellowship, breaking of bread, and prayer (Acts 2:42).

c. In church, prayer ranks as equal in importance with the teachings of the apostles (Acts 3:1; Acts 6:4).

V. **Prayer was *exemplified* by the Lord Jesus Christ.**

a. Definition of *exemplify*: to show or illustrate by example

b. Jesus had a habit of prayer. As the Son of Man on this earth, he was subjected to the same frustrations, temptations, joys and sorrows that affect us all today. Through prayer, Jesus received help and strength to accomplish the task He had been given while remaining sinless.

c. Jesus practiced prayer (Matthew 26:36; Mark 1:35; Luke 6:12; Luke 22:39, 41).

d. Jesus taught prayer (Matthew 6:9; Luke 11:1-4).

e. Jesus demonstrated prayer (Matthew 26:36-44; Mark 6:41; John 17:1-26).

f. Jesus intercedes for us in prayer (Romans 8:34).

VI. **Prayer *defeats* the devil.**

a. Definition of *defeat*: to win a victory over someone in battle

b. We have a spiritual (invisible) enemy. We are in a real spiritual battle and only spiritual weapons can get results. Prayer is a spiritual weapon. See Mark 9:29; II Corinthians 10:4; Ephesians 6:12 for scriptural evidence.

VII. **Prayer guards us from *sin*.**

a. Definition of sin: to transgress against God's law; to miss the mark

b. In times of temptation, Jesus taught that men should do two things: 1) watch, so that we pay attention and we will not be taken unawares (by surprise); and 2) pray that we don't enter into temptation. We should pay attention to what's going on in our lives, and the world around us. Then, we will know how to pray and what to pray for (Matthew 26:41; Luke 18:1; I John 3:4).

VIII. Prayer is *rewarded.*

    a. Definition of *reward:* a thing given in recognition of one's service, effort, or achievement

    b. Secret (closet) prayers, bring open rewards. Prayer is not time wasted; it is time invested (Matthew 6:6).

IX. Prayer is a faith *builder.*

    a. Definition of *build*: edifying, as a house builder or body builder; to construct

    b. We must pray by the enabling power of the Holy Spirit, which builds our faith in God. We have the responsibility of building our spirit, by praying in the Holy Ghost (Jude 1: 3, 20).

Other Reasons To Pray

• Prayer Saves the Sinner	Luke 11:13; Acts 10:2-4
• Prayer Sends Forth Laborers	Matthew 9:38
• Prayer Heals the Sick	I Kings 17:21-22; James 5:13-15
• Prayer Imparts Wisdom	James 1:5
• Prayer Brings Revelation	2 Kings 6:17; Jeremiah 33:3
• Prayer Helps One to Grow Spiritually	I Corinthians 14:2-4
• Prayer Bestows Peace	Philippians 4:6-7
• Prayer for Help	Hebrews 4:16
• Prayer to Meet Our Needs	Philippians 4:19

Summary

- Prayer is a commandment, not an option.

- We must acquire a serious life of prayer, or we will become spiritually weak!

- God gave mankind the authority to determine what happens on earth through prayer.

- God desires our fellowship, and by prayer we maintain our relationship with Him.

Lesson 3: They That Know Their God
Introduction

God desires our fellowship. Through prayer we maintain our relationship with Him. In order for a person to pray effectively, he needs to know the character and personality of the One whom he is petitioning. The more we know and understand the character and nature of the One to whom we pray, the more we will trust and believe in Him! We can know this God through prayer; but, we can also know God through His Word (reading the Bible, hearing preaching or teaching, or prophecy), through experience, or through direct inspiration.

"For my thoughts are not your thoughts, neither are your ways my ways, saith the Lord.

For as the heavens are higher than the earth, so are my ways higher than your ways, and my thoughts than your thoughts." **Isaiah 55:8-9**

God's thoughts and ways are not those of the natural man. Our prayers are hindered if we believe that we can fit God into our mold — to make his plans and purposes conform to ours.

"Thus saith the LORD, Let not the wise man glory in his wisdom, neither let the mighty man glory in his might, let not the rich man glory in his riches: But let him that glorieth, glory in this, that he understandeth and knoweth me, that I am the LORD which exercise lovingkindness, judgment, and righteousness, in the earth: for in these things I delight, saith the LORD."
Jeremiah 9:23-24

This verse from Jeremiah highlights the fact that all earthly values are insignificant when compared to the joy and excellency of knowing God.

"…but the people that do know their God shall be strong, and do exploits." **Daniel 11:32**

An unknown God can neither be trusted, served, nor worshipped. The foundation of all true knowledge of God must be a clear mental apprehension of His perfection as revealed in Holy Scripture.

"But without faith it is impossible to please him: for he that cometh to God must believe that he is, and that he is a rewarder of them that diligently seek him." **Hebrews 11:6**

We must believe in the existence of a personal, infinite, and holy God Who cares for us. Knowing God more via praying and studying/hearing His Word will enable us to know His will. (See I John 5:14-15). Knowing God when we pray will do the following: 1) enable us to please Him; 2) help us to praise Him; 3) help us to know His will; and 4) make our worship of Him more genuine.

Spiritual Activity

At this point, make a list of all the names of God that you know from memory. Do not seek help from the Bible or other references. Award yourself one point per name. Give yourself extra points if you know the scripture reference for each name!

25+ names	Highest Level	Excellent Job!
20 to 25	Intermediate Level	Good Job!
10 to 20	Moderate Level	Keep Going!
10 or less names	Beginner Level	Keep Trying!

They That Know Their God
Outline

The Characteristics of God

The more we know and understand the character and nature of the One to whom we pray, the more assurance we will have to believe His promises. Once we are informed regarding the character of God, we no longer have any excuse not to trust God (Philippians 3:10; II Peter 1:3)!

Non-Moral Characteristics

God is SPIRIT

He is immaterial and incorporeal (Luke 24:39). He is invisible (Colossians 1:15). He is alive (Revelation 1:18). He can ONLY be known spiritually (John 4:23-24).

God is CREATOR

God the Creator brought all things into existence out of nothing, *ex nihilo*, which means out of nothing. The word "created," is an activity that only God can do. God called into existence matter, substance, space, time, and all reality which had no prior existence (Genesis 1:1; Isaiah 40:28; Psalm 33:6, 9). God is distinct from His creation.

God is ONE

He is one God. He has manifested Himself to man in three ways: Father (in creation), Son (in redemption), and Holy Spirit (in the Church). Yet, not three, but ONE God (Deuteronomy 6:4; Ephesians 4:5-6; Colossians 2:8-9)!

God is ETERNAL

There was never a time, either in the past or the future, when God did not or will not exist. He is not bound by time. He has no beginning. He has no past, so he's not in the past. He has no future, so He's not in the future. Thus, He doesn't answer prayer in the future because God is ONLY in the present! God is, which is why He called Himself "I am" (not "was," or "will be"). (See Exodus 3:14; Psalm 90:2; Isaiah 40:28; and John 8:58 for further study.)

God is TRANSCENDENT

He is different and independent from His creation. His being and existence are infinitely greater and higher than the created order. He dwells in perfect and pure existence, far above what He has made. He Himself is uncreated and exists apart from creation, yet capable of dwelling among His people as their God (II Chronicles 2:6; Jeremiah 23:24).

God is OMNIPRESENT

He is present everywhere at the same time. No matter where we go, God is there. He observes everything we do (Psalm 139:7-12; Proverbs 15:3).

God is OMNISCIENT

He knows everything. He knows not only our actions, but also our thoughts. He knows past, present and future. He never learns anything (Psalm 139:1-6; Psalm 147:5; Isaiah 40:14, 28; Isaiah 46:9-13; John 1:48; Hebrews 4:13).

God is OMNIPOTENT

He is all-powerful and has ultimate authority over all things, and all creatures, including the following: nature, animals, sickness, disease, demons, and death (Psalm 62:11; Matthew 28:18; Hebrews 1:3)

God is IMMUTABLE

There is no changing in the attributes of God, in His perfection, or in His purpose for mankind. God is faithful to His own Word (Malachi 3:6; James 1:17; Hebrews 6:17-18; Hebrews 13:8).

God is PERFECT and HOLY

He is completely without sin and absolutely righteous. Adam and Eve were created without sin, but with the capability of sinning. God on the other hand CANNOT SIN. (Isaiah 6:1-3; I Peter 1:16; Matthew 5:48; Revelation 4:8)

Moral Characteristics

Many characteristics of the one true God, particularly His moral attributes, bear similarity to human qualities; however, His attributes all exist to a greater degree than they do in us.

God is GOOD

All that God originally created was good, an extension of His own nature. He continues to be good to His creation by sustaining His goodness to all of His creatures. (Psalm 100:5; Matthew 19:17; Galatians 5:22)

God is LOVE

God's love is a selfless love embracing the whole world of sinful humanity. The way He expressed His love was sending His only Son, Jesus, to die for sinners. (John 3:16; Galatians 5:22; I John 4:8-9)

God is MERCIFUL and GRACIOUS

His mercy keeps Him from giving us what we deserve, and His grace causes Him to give us what we don't deserve! God does not cut off and destroy humanity as is merited by our sins, but offers forgiveness as a free gift to be received through faith in Jesus Christ. (Lamentations 3:22; Ephesians 2:4, 8)

God is COMPASSIONATE

To be compassionate means to feel sorrow for someone else's suffering with a desire to help. (Lamentations 3:22; Mark 8:2; Luke 7:13; Luke 15:20; I Peter 3:8)

God is PATIENT and LONGSUFFERING

God is longsuffering with the sinful human race. He does not presently judge so as to destroy the world because he patiently gives everyone the opportunity to repent and be saved. (Numbers 14:18; Galatians 5:22; 2 Peter 3:9)

God is TRUTH

God is entirely trustworthy and true in all He says and does. His word is also described as truth. God does not tolerate lies or falsehood of any kind. (Deuteronomy 32:4; John 8:32; John 14:6; John 17:17; I John 5:6)

God is FAITHFUL

God will do what He has revealed in His Word, carrying out both His promises and His warnings. (Isaiah 55:11; I Corinthians 10:13; II Corinthians 1:20; Hebrews 10:23)

God is JUST

To be just means that God upholds the moral order of the universe, and is righteous and without sin in the manner in which He treats mankind. God's determination to punish sinners with death proceeds from His justice. He reveals His wrath against every form of wickedness. He loves righteousness and hates evil. (Psalm 7:11; Isaiah 45:21-25; John 5:30; Romans 1:18; Romans 6:23)

God's final revelation of Himself is in Jesus Christ. God came to reveal Himself in a person. If we want to know what God is like, we look at Jesus (Hebrews 1:1-3).

Summary

- An unknown God can neither be trusted, served, nor worshipped.

- God's final revelation of Himself is in Jesus Christ.

- Knowing and understanding the character and nature of the One to Whom we pray will:

    o   enable us to trust and believe in Him;

    o   help us to sincerely praise Him and make our worship of Him more genuine; and

    o   help us to know His will.

Lesson 4: Lord, Teach Me To Pray
Introduction

Note: There are a variety of different patterns of prayer taught in and/or supported by the Bible. The purpose here is to present one of those patterns: what is commonly known as the Lord's Prayer. In the outline, we present well known components of prayer gleaned from other passages of Scripture.

Comprehensive knowledge of how to pray is not an innate attribute of mankind. It is surprising to know that many believers do not know how to pray, and many others have no desire to pray. However, I do believe that if more parents would commit themselves to training and disciplining their children to pray, we could have a generation of young, praying people (see Proverbs 22:6). In this text, the Hebrew word translated as *train up* means *to dedicate* or *to discipline*. Therefore, parents must cultivate within their children a taste for prayer. They should endeavor to inspire within their children a desire to seek God for themselves, and thus enjoy genuine spiritual experiences with God.

...one of his disciples said unto him, Lord teach us to pray, as John also taught his disciples.
Luke 11:1

The true method of praying can be learned only through being a student of prayer. The disciples took notice of Jesus' prayers. They were awestruck with the fervor and effectiveness of the Lord's prayers. Remembering that John the Baptist taught his disciples to pray, Jesus' disciples also asked Him to teach them to pray. We too, should say, "Lord, teach me to pray!"

In response, Jesus gave His disciples, and us, a pattern to follow in prayer. This prayer is a sketch, or a blueprint, for Christians to follow as they pray to God. We are to develop these points as we pray. When we learn to pray the way that Jesus taught His disciples to pray, we can pray longer and better.

As we learn to follow the plan Jesus gave us, our prayer life will no longer be a frustrating puzzle; instead, our time in prayer will become easy and natural. Our primary goals in prayer are the following: to begin to move into the presence of God; to understand the character and purposes of God; and to spend quality time with God!

Seven Elements of the Lord's Prayer (Luke 11:1-4)

1. Personal Relationship – "Our Father which art in heaven"

2. Praise & Worship – "Hallowed be thy name"

3. Expectation – "Thy kingdom come"

4. Submission/Authority – "Thy will be done, as in heaven, so in earth"

5. Petition – "Give us day by day our daily bread"

6. Forgiveness – "And forgive us our sins; as we forgive everyone that is indebted to us"

7. Deliverance – "And lead us not into temptation; but deliver us from evil"

These are the areas of concern of our Lord Jesus Christ that should occupy our prayers. These elements should be included in our personal prayers and in our corporate prayers.

Lord, Teach Me To Pray
Outline

Note: Each component is a prayer in itself and can be prayed individually or in any combination.

I. **Acknowledgement of God** (Matthew 6:8-9; John 16:23; Romans 8:15)

II. **The Prayer of Thanksgiving**

    A. An attitude of gratefulness for what God has done for you. (Psalm 100:4; I Thessalonians 5:18)

    B. Remembering what He has done (Psalm 63:6-7; Psalm 77:11-12; Psalm 103:2)

    C. Don't be unthankful (Luke 17:16-19; II Timothy 3:1-2)

III. **The Prayer of Praise**

    A. A physical expression of thankfulness to God. (Psalm 47:1; Psalm 149:3; Acts 3:8)

    B. To magnify, and to glorify Him. (Psalm 34:3; Psalm 150:6)

    C. Praise is NOT silent! (Isaiah 38:18)

IV. **The Prayer of Repentance**

    A. Godly sorrow for offending God (Romans 2:4; II Corinthians 7:10)

    B. Intent to turn and change direction (Psalm 51:1-19)

V. **The Prayer of Confession**

    A. A declaration of guilt; to admit sin

        1. Negative Confession (Joshua 7:19; Proverbs 28:13; James 5:16; I John 1:8-10).

B. A declaration of God's Word

    1. Positive Confession (Romans 10:9-10; II Corinthians 4:13)

VI.   The Prayer of Petition/Supplication

A. Petition is a request; asking God to meet a need or desire (I Samuel 1:9-11 (Hannah); Jeremiah 33:3; Matthew 7:7-8; John 14:13-14; Philippians 4:6)

B. Petition must align with God's will (I John 5:14-15)

C. Petition for God's glory to be manifested (John 14:13)

VII.   The Prayer of Intercession

A. To approach the Almighty God on behalf of another, with compassion, pleading for mercy and help (Genesis 18:23-33 (Abraham); Numbers 12:13 (Moses); Ezekiel 22:30; Romans 8:26)

VIII.   The Prayer of Worship

A. To bow down, to kiss; prostrate oneself; to honor and adore (John 4:22-24)

B. It's all about God in heaven! (Isaiah 6:1-4; Revelation 4:8-11; 5:11-14)

    1. worship has nothing to do with us

    2. worship has nothing to do with what we need

    3. worship has nothing to do with our circumstances

    4. worship has nothing to do with how good He's been to us

    5. worship does have everything to do with our sacrifice and obedience to God (Romans 12:1 - "your reasonable service" in this text means your reasonable worship)

Summary

- Comprehensive knowledge of how to pray is not an innate attribute of mankind.

- The true method of praying can be learned only through being a student of prayer.

- Elements of prayer can be prayed individually or in any combination.

- When we learn to pray the way that Jesus taught His disciples to pray, we can pray longer and better.

Lesson 5: Daily, I Shall Worship Thee
Introduction

"Thou wilt shew me the path of life: in thy presence is fullness of joy; at thy right hand there are pleasures for evermore." **Psalm 16:11**

The goal of the prayer of worship is to bring us into the presence of God. In God's presence, we feel completeness, unworthiness, and satisfying joy.

"God is Spirit: and they that worship him must worship him in spirit and in truth." **John 4:24**

Since God is Spirit, our communication with Him must be through the Holy Spirit. True worship is communion with God's Spirit and our spirit becoming one.

God seeks worship and *worshippers* — people who are committed, submitted, and dedicated to rendering worship to Him. God created us to have daily communion with Him. He wants a relationship with someone who, of their own free will, desires to be with Him. He has never forced anyone to be with Him, and He never will because He is love. The Father desires that we make the decision to be with Him because that is what we want. It is sad to think the God of the universe, the creator of heaven and earth, has to seek for worshippers (John 4:23)!

Many believers may never get into His presence, because they don't know *how* to worship. Worship takes us to a higher place, where the Holy Spirit moves and works. In worship we are brought into harmony with God's divine purposes. Through worship we become more Christ-like as we have fellowship with Him. Through worship, we can place ourselves on a trajectory towards being filled with all the fullness of God (Ephesians 3:19)!

In prayer is where I learned to worship God. Psalm 100 gives us a pattern for worship which I use in prayer. I call Psalms 100, the prayer of worship. It gives us the formula of how to enter into the presence of God to worship.

So, I no longer rise early in the morning just to make petitions to God, or to take a list of prayer requests. I rise early to worship the living God! There's no one there, except me and Him. In worship, I start my day feeling His presence stirring and energizing my spirit on the inside. I can feel my spirit being refilled, giving me new life! Early in the morning, my body doesn't want to get up much less pray! My emotions are weak, but my spirit is willing! When my prayer is ended, my spirit, indeed, is edified (see Jude 1:20)! What a great way to start the day!

Song: **"Daily I Shall Worship Thee"**

Daily I shall worship Thee,

Lamb of God who died for me,

He extended endless mercies,

Daily I shall worship Thee

Author: unknown

Daily, I Shall Worship Thee
Outline

This outline will examine Psalm 100:1-4, which contains a pattern that will lead us into the presence of the Lord. Rising early in the morning to seek the Lord, to seek His presence, and to build an everlasting relationship with the Father is our purpose (Psalm 5:3). Instead of taking petitions and interceding for others, the only focus in this prayer is to get the Lord's attention through singing, thanksgiving, praise, and blessing His name. These four aspects should usher us into worship, where we encounter His presence.

The Prayer of Worship

This Prayer:

- Excludes petition and intercession

- **Gives** to God, instead of **receiving** from Him

- Gets God's Attention, because it's about Him

- Stops mind-wandering

- Silences the devil, which causes him to flee

I. **Make a joyful noise unto the Lord** – Psalm 100:1

- "joyful noise" means: to sound loud; outcry; open your mouth with praise

- Act like you're at the ballgame and Jesus is winning the game! (Psalm 47:1; Psalm 55:17; Psalm 95:1-2)

- This noise releases pressure within you and breaks up negative atmosphere; this noise can include your voice and/or clapping.

II. **Come before His presence with singing** – Psalm 100:2

- Sing songs to the Lord in prayer in the morning (Psalm 104:33; Acts 16:25; Ephesians. 5:19; Colossians 3:16)

III. **Enter into His gates with thanksgiving** – Psalm 100:4

God desires thankfulness from His people. How many things can you thank Him for?

- Thankfulness is missing in the last days (2 Timothy 3:1-2)

- Thankfulness is the will of God (I Thessalonians 5:18)

- Thankfulness shows faith (Luke 17:16)

- Thankfulness delivers (Jonah 2:1-10)

IV. **Enter into His courts with praise** – Psalm 100:4

God inhabits the praises of His people! Put on a garment of Praise!

- Praise gets God's attention (Isaiah 6:4; Mark 10:48; Acts 4:31)

- Praise changes the atmosphere (Acts 16:25)

- Praise magnifies the Lord (Psalm 34:3)

- Praise lifts the spirit of heaviness/depression (Isaiah 61:3)

V. **Bless His name (with Worship)** – Psalm 100:4

Bless His name means to praise, adore, and salute His name!

- Do you know God? Can you bring in His Presence? Psalm 16:11

- How do you define God? What names can you call Him?

- What scriptures can you quote for those names of God?

Even heaven worships: Isaiah 6:1-4; Revelation 4:8.

Note: Practice all of these principles in a group prayer session.

Summary

- The goal of the prayer of worship is to bring us into the presence of God.

- Since God is Spirit, our communication with Him must be through the Holy Spirit.

- The prayer of worship excludes petitions and interceding for others.

- The prayer of worship should usher us into God's presence through: singing, thanksgiving, praise, and blessing His name.

Lesson 6: A Living Sacrifice
Introduction

Sacrifice has been linked to worship since God formally instituted the Jewish sacrificial system in Exodus. As a means of temporarily dealing with their sin, Israel was instructed to publically worship God by making a sacrifice - typically an animal sacrifice. Even before the sacrificial system of worship was formally instituted, it was a part of life for the Jewish patriarchs (see Genesis 22:1-18).

This sacrificial worship foreshadowed Jesus Christ, the Lamb of God Who would take away the sins of the world (John 1:29) by His sacrificial death on the cross! In the ultimate act of worship, Jesus submitted to the will of His Father and willingly subjected Himself to die a heinous death in our stead (Romans 5:12-21). This sacrifice of His human life was made possible primarily through daily sacrificial prayer (and never-ending dialogue) with the Father in which Jesus communed with the Father. If Jesus could sacrifice His life, will you not sacrifice sleep/food/family time/entertainment?

Whereas Jesus sacrificed His physical life for us through His death on the cross, He is merely requiring for saints to sacrifice our lives by giving ourselves over to Him in this life on earth. This is where the injunction from Paul in Romans 12:1 is pertinent. Here, Paul admonishes the saints to, "...present your bodies a living sacrifice, holy, acceptable unto God, which is your reasonable service." The act of giving ourselves over to God's divine plan is what is meant by a *living sacrifice*, as most saints will not be required to die physically for our faith, but all saints are required to *die to ourselves.* Sacrificial prayer is one way to demonstrate our love for our Savior: Jesus Christ. Moreover, there is a reward for sacrifices made by saints, as can be gleaned from Mark 10:28-30, where Jesus promises pronounced sacrifices are linked to abundant earthly and heavenly rewards.

So the next time you want to hit the snooze button, consider Calvary. The next time you wrestle mentally with the idea of praying before sunrise, consider Gethsemane (see Luke 22:39-45). The next time you wonder why sacrificial prayer is vital, consider how His flesh was shredded by the cat-o-nine-tails. More than this, remember: you are not doing God a favor through sacrificial prayer. You are solely helping yourself, positioning yourself to be more like Jesus! Here the words of Ezra T. Benson ring true for every saint: "He who (first) kneels before God can stand before anyone!"

A Living Sacrifice
Outline

Sacrifice means to give up something of value for something of greater value. Everything we can possibly value - comfort, food, sleep, job, entertainment, relationships etc. - is well worth sacrificing to obtain quality time with our Savior (Romans 12:1)!

The foundation of Jesus' effectiveness in ministry was His private prayer. Private prayer must be the foundation of your ministry too. You cannot expect to be more effective in ministry, without spending time in daily prayer (Acts 4:13).

I.   **Early Morning Prayer**

    a. Rising before daybreak (between 3 am and 6 am)

       Psalm 5:3; Proverbs 8:17; Mark 1:35

    b. To meet God first: before the shower, before breakfast, before coffee

       Psalm 63:1; Matthew 6:33

    c. To maintain a level of consistency

       Daniel 6:10; Luke 22:39; Acts 3:1

    d. Less distractions

       Luke 21:34-36

    e. Gain more anointing

       Exodus 34:29-35; Luke 9:28-29; Jude 1:20

    f. Ask God for prayer time, if you don't have one

II.   **Finding the Secret Place** (in the home)

Daniel 6:10; Matthew 6:6

    a. Do not pray at the bedside

    b. Do not pray in the dark

        1. There was a continual light in the tabernacle (see Leviticus 24:1-4)

    c. Pray this prayer alone

        1. Matthew 26:36; Luke 5:16; Luke 9:18

    d. Pray out loud, (wash face if necessary) Psalm 55:17

III.   **Begin With Twenty Minutes** (20 min.)

    a. **Persistence** will increase length of time in prayer

        1. Even Jesus had a habit of prayer (Luke 22:39)

            a. "Wont" in Luke 22:39 means habit.

    b. Goal to reach *one hour* of prayer

        1. Matthew 26:40

    b. Begin with praise and worship (see: *Prayer of Worship*)

        1. Psalm 100:4

Month _____

Year _____

Instructions

This is a sample Sacrificial Prayer Chart for students of prayer. This chart is designed to allow the student to participate in prayer while receiving teachings on prayer. The student should chart their daily prayer time. The prayer time is between 3 am and 6 am. The duration of your prayer is to be determined by the instructor. Beginners should aim for 20 min. per day and graduate to 1 hour per day. When prayer time is missed or late, record it. At the end of the month the prayer chart should be turned in and graded or rewarded by the instructor.

Sunday	Monday	Tuesday	Wednesday	Thursday	Friday	Saturday
Bible Reading – B Fasting - F			Start Time Finish Time Total Time	2 5:00 am 5:45 am 45 min. Total	3	4
5	6	7	8	9	10	11
12	13	14	15	16	17	18
19	20	21	22	23	24	25
26	27	28	29	30		

Name: _____

Summary

- Sacrificial prayer is one way to demonstrate our love for our Savior Jesus Christ.

- Rising for early morning prayer is presenting our bodies as a living sacrifice.

- We must set a time and place to meet God daily.

- Sacrifices to God in prayer are always rewarded.

Lesson 7: Give Me A Praying Spirit
Introduction

What is the Spirit? Or more accurately, Who is the Spirit? The answer to this question helps to substantiate why and how a believer prays in the Spirit. The Spirit, Holy Spirit, Holy Ghost, or His Spirit are all synonymous terms. These terms all refer to the Spirit of God. The Spirit of God is God Himself. The Spirit is the spirit of truth and He is the Comforter Who comes alongside a child of God and helps them make it from this life to Heaven (John 15:26).

According to Proverbs 20:27, mankind was created with a human spirit. This is distinct from, yet related to, the Holy Spirit. Once an individual is born again or born from above according to John 3:5 and Acts 2:38, this person now has a new, indwelling, life-giving, divine spirit that now is linked to the Holy Spirit. As can be gleaned from Mark 2:22, we receive a new supernatural spirit (new wineskin), which is then filled with the infinite Holy Spirit (new wine).

Having the abiding presence of the Holy Spirit within one's mortal body will enable the believer to pray in the Spirit, which is praying in tongues (see Acts 2:1-4). Through prayer in tongues, the believer can pray the perfect will of God concerning any situation! Prayer in the Spirit can also occur in one's native language when that prayer is inspired by the Holy Spirit.

This divine spirit can serve as a conduit through which the soul can be transformed daily by the Holy Spirit as the believer prays in the Spirit. Once a person is Spirit-filled, they automatically have a praying spirit, because they have the same spirit that compelled Jesus, Who always prayed.

Give Me A Praying Spirit
Outline

Praying in the Spirit is a prayer that enables the power of the Holy Ghost to inspire, guide, energize, empower us to maintain a holy life, and help us to do battle in our prayers. Many church leaders have failed to teach this important doctrine to believers, even though it is mentioned at least three times in the New Testament (Romans 8:26; Ephesians 6:18; Jude 1:20).

Praying In The Spirit Principles

- **Being Born of the Spirit**

    - First, you must be born of the spirit (John 3:1-8)

    - How to receive the Holy Spirit - repentance (Acts 2:38)

    - You must have the initial evidence of the Holy Spirit, which is speaking in tongues as God enables (Acts 2:4)

    - You are not a son of God without the Holy Spirit (Romans 8:9, 11, 14, 16)

    - True worship is in the Spirit (John 4:22-24)

- **Speaking in Tongues: A Heavenly Language Given by God**

    - This language came from heaven. (John 1:32; Acts 2:2; I Peter 1:12)

    - This language ought to be spoken daily. (I Corinthians 14:2, 4, 18)

    - This language is under the influence of the Holy Spirit, bypassing the brain and human thought. (I Corinthians 14:14-15)

- **Intercedes in Prayer**

  - Sometimes we don't know what to pray for or how to pray. The Holy Spirit is involved in our intercession; The Spirit knows the mind of God and can pray His will (Romans 8:26-27, 34).

  - Christ intercedes for the believer in heaven (Hebrews 7:25); and the Holy Spirit intercedes within the believer on earth.

- **Spiritual Weapon**

  - We are in a *spiritual* battle and the devil and his demons are our spiritual foes (Ephesians 6:12).

  - The believer's warfare against satan's spiritual forces calls for an intensity in prayer.

  - Spiritual warfare is fighting against evil spiritual forces whose intent is to hinder us from receiving all of the promises of God.

  - Praying in the Spirit is an instrument of offense and defense, designed for destroying the enemy and protecting us from his attacks.

- **The Spirit Gives Us Revelation**

  - It is only through the Holy Spirit that God's truth and wisdom are revealed to humanity (II Kings 6:15-17; I Corinthians 2:9-14).

  - The Holy Spirit fully knows the thoughts of God (I Corinthians 2:11).

- **Praise and Magnify God**

  - Speaking in tongues can involve praise and magnifying God (Acts 2:11; Acts 10:46)

- God dwells in the midst of praise. Praise ushers us into His presence. (Psalm 22:3; Psalm 100:4)

7. Builds Faith

- It's the believer's *individual responsibility* to edify themselves in their faith, through *prayer in the Holy Ghost*.

- In Jude 1:20, we are admonished to pray in the Holy Ghost, as a remedy to the end-time apostasy.

Prayer in the Spirit may be prayer in your native language, with the Holy Ghost providing direction and revelation as you pray. It may also be prayer in an unknown tongue, where the Holy Ghost by-passes your brain and mind, and you do not understand what you are saying. Either way, this type of prayer is *supernaturally empowered* and is always in accordance with *the will of God*. Praying in tongues will cause your *faith to come alive*, with boldness and supernatural power!

Today, "*Be Filled with the Holy Spirit*". Everyday, "Be Re-Filled with the Holy Spirit".

Summary

- Praying in the Spirit, praying in the Holy Ghost, and praying in tongues are synonymous.

- In order for one to pray in the Holy Spirit, one must have the indwelling of the Holy Spirit with the evidence of speaking in tongues.

- Speaking in tongues is a heavenly language given by God to pray in the Spirit.

- Praying in the Spirit enables the power of the Holy Spirit to: inspire us in the things of God; guide us in our walk with God; energize our spirit with spiritual strength; and help us engage in spiritual battle in prayer.

Lesson 8: Hindrances To Prayer
Introduction

While the Bible teaches us that mankind can enjoy the blessedness of direct and continual access to God in prayer, it must be noted that there are a variety of factors that can hinder this access. These hindrances to prayer that are outlined in this lesson can be categorized into two main categories: blatant sinful hindrances and more subtle hindrances (weights).

In order to better grasp the distinctions, let us examine the text. *Wherefore seeing we also are compassed about with so great a cloud of witnesses, let us lay aside every weight, and the sin which doth so easily beset us, and let us run with patience the race that is set before us,* (Hebrews 12:1). First, it's important to realize that the writer of Hebrews is utilizing a sport (racing) metaphorically in order to convey his/her points concerning sin and weights. The writer compares the Christian lifestyle to a race, which we must "run with patience." During races of that period in Rome, runners raced either completely or nearly naked so as to minimize obstructions to their movement.

This flows right into the next key point. We must observe that just as runners of that day did not run while wearing cumbersome clothing, so too must the Christian live without hindrances to his/her prayer life. We can reasonably infer that weights are sins; they're just more subtle sins. The term weight is translated from a Greek term, Ogkos, which means "whatever is prominent, protuberance, bulk, mass; hence a burden, weight, encumbrance." Wearing clothes during these ancient races was not, in of itself wrong; however, doing so hindered the runners' ability to run. For example, one's love for their spouse is not wrong in itself, but this love can become a weight if it surpasses one's love for God. These hindrances can have deadly consequences. For instance, Adam lost God's presence through his disobedience in Eden. Therefore, the Christian is instructed to shed every weight that hinders impediment to their progress in their prayer life.

Weights and sin both hinder every aspect of the Christian lifestyle. The sin/weight issue can be effectively addressed through repentance. Finally, these hindrances can also be deadly in that they can cause God to turn a deaf ear to our prayers (Isaiah 59:1-2).

Hindrances To Prayer
Outline

1. **Disobedience** (Genesis 3:11; I Samuel 15:14, 22)

   - Definition, Webster's 1828: neglect or refusal to obey; violation of a command

   - God gave man the freedom to choose to obey or disobey. Disobeying God's command is sin. (James 4:17; I John 3:4)

   - Sin separates us from fellowship with God. (Isaiah 59:1-2)

2. **Secret/Unconfessed Sin** (Joshua 7:19-20; Proverbs 28:13)

   - Definition, Webster's 1828: concealed from the knowledge of all persons except the individual; private, hid

   - No one can ever hide their sins from God, Who is omniscient. However, confessing our sins and forsaking iniquity allows prosperity and God's mercy to work in our lives (Hebrew 4:13).

3. **Refusing to Forgive** (Matthew 5:23-24; Matthew 6:14-15; Matthew 18:15-17; Luke 17:3-4)

   - Definition, Webster's 1828: to pardon; to overlook an offense, and treat the offender as not guilty.

   - Unforgiveness is the reason many people do not receive healing, deliverance, or answers to their prayers. Forgiveness is not a feeling, it is a choice. True forgiveness is acting like it never happened (Hagin, 1983).

4. **Marriage Relationships** (I Peter 3:7)

- Definition, Webster's 1828: state of being related by kindred

- Peter indicates that a husband who fails to live with his wife in an understanding way and to give her honor as a fellow child of God will damage his relationship with God by creating a barrier between his prayers and God. (The Full Life Study Bible)

5. **Doubt/Unbelief** (Mark 6:5-6; Luke 1:20; Romans 4:19-22; James 1:5-8)

- Definition, Webster 1828: doubt, to waiver or fluctuate in opinion; to be in uncertainty; unbelief, disbelief of divine revelation

- A doubter is genuinely seeking for the truth in a given situation and wondering if an answer really exists. When the answer is revealed to a doubter, because of the seeking nature of his heart, the doubter will be open to accepting the truth and appropriating it in his life (Breakthrough Covenant Partner Devotional Bible).

- Someone with unbelief is not as easily convinced. He firmly believes that what he knows is the absolute truth, and there could never be any other answer. The unbeliever has placed judgment on what God can and cannot do, thus limiting his ability to receive from God (Breakthrough Covenant Partner Devotional Bible).

6. **Refusing Biblical Teaching** (Proverbs 28:9)

- Definition, Webster 1828: teach, to instruct, to deliver any doctrine

- God will not answer the prayers of those who have no sincere commitment to obey Him and His word. Prayer without love for God's Word and law is hypocrisy and is insulting to Him. (The Full Life Study Bible)

7. **Fear** (II Timothy 1:7; I John 4:18)

- Definition: The expectation of immediate danger or threat.

- Fear is the enemy of faith. Fear is the opposite of faith.

- Fear is not of God. It is of the devil. God will not move on your behalf when you are fearful.

Other Hindrances To Prayer

- **Busyness** (Luke 10:38-42)

- **Laziness** (Proverbs 13:4)

- **Poor Planning** (Ephesians 5:15-16 GW)

- **Ignorance** (Hosea 4:6; I Corinthians 14:38)

- **Love for Pleasure** (II Timothy 3:4)

- **Lack of Desire** (Revelation 3:15-17)

- **satan** (John 10:10; I Peter 5:8)

Summary

- Sin will cause God not to hear our prayers!

- No one can ever hide their sins from God.

- Unforgiveness is a hindrance that causes people not to receive healing, deliverance, or answers to their prayers.

- Confession and repentance from sin brings restoration so that God will once again hear our prayers.

Lesson 9: Don't Stop Praying
Introduction

"And he spake a parable unto them to this end, that men ought always to pray, and not to faint" (**Luke 18:1 KJV**). There are two reasons that we should continue in prayer. The first reason is that God commands His people to pray, and to keep praying until Jesus Christ returns, no matter how long He tarries. Due to satan and the pleasures of this world, many will cease to have a persistent prayer life. Truly, we are living in perilous times, when it's no longer popular to be faithful to church, to read the scriptures, and much less to spend time in prayer. Saints, please, don't stop praying!

"Jesus used this illustration with His disciples to show them that they need to pray always and never give up" (**Luke 18:1 GW**). A daily, persistent prayer life is absolutely necessary for God's will to be accomplished in our lives. Believers are to develop a consistent time of prayer, to maintain an unbroken relationship with God, to practice entering the presence of God, and to walk in a constant state of prayer.

The second reason that we should continue in prayer is because sometimes we do not receive the answers to our prayers immediately. "One day Jesus told his disciples a story to illustrate their need for constant prayer and to show them that they must keep praying until the answer comes" (**Luke 18:1 TLB**).

God desires to communicate with His people, and He promises to answer our prayers. However, He doesn't always answer immediately or when we desire. God hears our prayers, and He promises to answer prayer (see Jeremiah 33:3).We must ask in prayer, seek if necessary, and keep on knocking relentlessly until He answers (see Matthew 7:7-8). Don't Stop Praying!

Song: Saints Don't Stop Praying

Saints, don't stop praying, for the Lord is nigh.

Saints, don't stop praying, He'll hear your cry.

For the Lord has promised, His word is true.

Just don't stop praying, He'll answer you!

Author: Edna Randolph Worrell

Finally, the scripture text says: "And he spake a parable unto them to this end, that men ought always to pray, and not to faint" (**Luke 18:1 KJV**). The last clause in this verse carries a serious warning that if God's people fail to continue in a life of prayer, they will faint (to be weak or fail spiritually)! Without a daily life of prayer, we will fail in all areas of our spiritual life. Prayer is not an option or a choice; it is essential to our very lives as saints. If Jesus had to pray, what about His people? If we plan to make it to heaven and desire to remain victorious in our walk with God, we must practice a life of prayer.

A consistent, persistent life of prayer begins at home. Our day should begin with prayer. Make your home a house of prayer. Parents, set an example of prayer, and teach your children how to pray. Pray in the morning. Pray throughout the day. Pray in the evening, and pray at the end of the day. Saints, please, don't stop praying!

Don't Stop Praying
Outline

Two Types Of Persistent Prayer

- Continual personal prayer (Luke 18:1; Hebrews 11:6)

- Continual prayer concerning prayers yet to be answered

  - The Midnight Caller (Luke 11:5-10); Persistent Widow (Luke 18:2-8)

Why Persistence Is Necessary

I. Unseen Spiritual Battles (Daniel 9:3; Daniel 10:12-13)

- The Christian life is a life of warfare. Our enemy and our battle is spiritual, not physical.

- God allows satan a limited ability to conduct spiritual warfare against us.

- Satan may even be allowed to hinder God's answers to our prayers, as seen in the book of Daniel.

- A materialistic, rational worldview hinders our recognition of our enemy's true nature.

II. Discovering God's Will (Matthew 26:36-44)

- Persistence in prayer requires us to bring the human will into submission to God's will, His way, and His timing.

- We must persist in prayer because of our own unreadiness to properly respond to the answer God has for us.

- We call this period "waiting on God".

  - God calls it, "waiting on us."

- He is waiting for us to be *transformed in character*, so He can entrust us with the answer.

- If God always gave us what we wanted when we wanted it, our inability to properly handle His answer would cause disaster.

III. **Testing Of Our Faith** (Matthew 15:22-28; I Peter 1:7)

- In persistent prayer, God uses the time of waiting to test our faith, sincerity, and desire.

- God rewards us with answered prayer when we diligently seek Him (Hebrews 11:6).

- If it's really important to us, we'll do whatever is necessary to get the answer.

- If it's not important to us, it won't be important to God.

Biblical Examples Of Persistence

- Jacob (Genesis 32:26)

- Elijah prays for rain (I Kings 17:1; I Kings 18:1, 41-45; James 5:17)

- Canaanite woman (Matthew 15:22-28)

- Jesus at Gethsemane (Matthew 26:36-44)

- Zacharias prays for a child (Luke 1:5-7, 13)

- Jesus heals a blind man (Mark 8:22-26)

- Cornelius (Acts 10:1-4, 31)

Saints, Keep Praying…

- Until God tells us, "Yes", "No", or "Wait";

- Until the burden is lifted.

Summary

- Due to satan and the pleasures of this world, many will cease to have a persistent prayer life.

- In persistent prayer, God uses the time of waiting to test our faith, sincerity, and desire.

- Saints, keep praying until: God tells us "Yes," "No," or "Wait"; or until the burden is lifted.

Lesson 10: A Praying Church
Introduction

The previous lessons have concentrated on a relationship with God through a personal prayer life. However, in this last lesson we change course and focus on the corporate prayer of the Church. The house of God is biblically called the "house of prayer". Prayer is one of the primary ministries of the Church (Acts 2:42). As such, prayer should be the passion of the pastor and other leaders of the local church; therefore, they will encourage and participate in corporate prayer. Whenever God's people gather together in unity, the greater number of saints, the greater the power to counter satan's opposition. Indeed, where there is unity in corporate prayer, blessings follow (Psalm 133:1-3).

There are a variety of questions that we must ask ourselves concerning the corporate prayer of the local place of worship. Are the Church's prayers answered? Are the petitions made in-line with God's Word? Do we receive the promised results? Do we allow time for testimonies of answered prayers? Do we from time to time, see the manifestations of our prayer requests immediately or miraculously? Do our corporate requests reflect God's agenda or our own personal interests? Are the requests urgent needs, or are they challenges that the Church may be facing now or in the future? Are we praying in unison for big requests to God that only He can fulfill? If we offer honest answers to these questions it will reveal the effectiveness (or lack thereof) of corporate prayer.

Prayer is the vehicle by which God has designed for His people to get things accomplished on earth. We have the power to bring heaven's blessing to earth (Matthew 6:10). Sometimes it only takes one prayer. Sometimes it takes many prayers over the course of years. Yet, let us persevere as God has promised to answer our prayers (Jeremiah 33:3; Matthew 7:7-8)! People of God, don't stay home! Go to the Holy Ghost Prayer Meeting and pray! The spiritual atmosphere of God's house is fortified by corporate prayer.

My hope is that this final lesson will charge the Church, the body of Christ, to revive our corporate prayer meeting with fire of the Holy Ghost, with expectation of God's promises, and with the confirmation of signs and wonders for God's glory!

A Praying Church
Outline

I.   **The Prayer of Agreement** (Matthew 18:19-20)

- **The Requirement:**

  - Two or three in agreement (in harmony regarding a matter), on earth.

  - In Jesus' name

- **The Request**:

  - Touching (concerning) anything (a thing), that they shall ask.

  - Unlimited petition (a formal request)

- **The Promise:**

  - It shall be done of the Father, in heaven.

  - The Lord's presence

II.   **An Apostolic Prayer Meeting** (Acts 4:23-31)

a. **Background** - After being arrested, threatened, and released for preaching Jesus and healing in His name, Peter and John went to corporate prayer instead of going home.

b. **Prayer was the response to the persecution and threats against the Church.**

- They lifted their voices to God. (Acts 4:24)

- With one accord, *homo-thumadon (same passion)* (Acts 1:14)

- They were in the same place, at the same time, with the same passion and emotion about the same thing!

c. **Acknowledgement of God.**

- The Lord, as God, the Creator. (Acts 4:24)

d. **The Prayer for Boldness**

- The disciples needed a renewal of their courage to witness and speak for Jesus, no matter the abuse or opposition (The Preacher's Outline and Sermon Bible).

- They asked to be "bold" witnesses of Christ in the face of fierce opposition (II Timothy 1:7; I John 4:18)

- We do not read that they were fearful, depressed, discouraged, or worried (The Preacher's Outline and Sermon Bible).

- They did not pray for their enemies to be destroyed, for the persecution to stop, nor for God to allow them to stop witnessing until things quieted down (The Preacher's Outline and Sermon Bible).

e. **The Prayer for Healing and Miracles**

- Only one thing can prove the validity of the gospel message: the power of the living Christ demonstrated in signs and wonders! (Mark 16:15-20)

f. **The Results of the Church's Unified Prayer**

- This prayer got God's attention; the results were immediate, and miraculous.

- **The Place Was Shaken**

  o To strike awe upon them, to awaken and raise their expectations, to give a token that God was with them, and to show them reason to fear God more, and fear man less (Isaiah 6:4; Acts 16:26; Henry, 1706)

- **All filled with the Holy Ghost**

  o To be "*filled with the Holy Ghost*," is to be influenced by the Spirit.

  o Unlike the "*indwelling*," of the Holy Spirit, it is a *repeated experience*.

  o We must receive constant "*re-fillings*," which are necessary for salvation and our ministry serving the Lord. (Ephesians 5:18)

- **Immediately, they received the boldness for which they had prayed!**

Summary

- Prayer is one of the primary ministries of the Church.

- God's House of Prayer needs to be continually fortified with prayer.

- Prayer must be a passion of the church leaders.

- Whenever two or three believers are gathered together in His name in harmonious prayer, Jesus promises: the Father will grant whatever they request; the Lord's presence will be there.

References

Dunn, R. (1992). Don't just stand there, pray something. Thomas Nelson Publishers. Nashville, TN.

Hagin, K. (1983). Unforgiveness. Faith Library Publications. Tulsa, OK.

Henry, M. (1706). Commentary on Acts.

Jones, C. (1997). The Prayer clinic manual. Bethesda Ministries. Cincinnati, OH.

Leadership Ministries Worldwide. (1992). The Preacher's outline and sermon bible. Alpha Omega Ministries, Inc.

Monroe, M. (2002). Understanding the purpose and power of prayer. Whittaker House. New Kensington, PA.

Stamps, D. C. (Ed.) (1992). The Full life study bible, King James Version. Zondervan. Grand Rapids, MI.

Made in the USA
Columbia, SC
17 August 2024

40602335R10037